F. SCOTT FITZGERALD

The Beautiful and Damned

Retold by Margaret Tarner

D1471955

MACMILLAN

CLASSICS

Level 2

INTERMEDIATE LEVEL

Founding Editor: John Milne

Macmillan Guided Readers provide a choice of enjoyable reading material for all learners of English. The series comprises three categories: MODERNS, CLASSICS and ORIGINALS. Macmillan **Moderns** are retold versions of popular and contemporary novels, published at four levels of grading – Beginner, Elementary, Intermediate and Upper. At **Intermediate Level**, the control of content and language has the following main features:

Information Control
Information vital to the understanding of the story is presented in an easily assimilated manner and is repeated when necessary. Difficult allusion and metaphor are avoided and cultural backgrounds are made explicit.

Structure Control
Most structures used in the Readers will be familiar to students who have completed an elementary course of English. Other grammatical features may occur, but their use is made clear through context and reinforcement. This ensures that the reading is enjoyable and provides a continual learning situation for the students. Sentences are limited in most cases to a maximum of three clauses and within sentences there is a balance of adverbial and adjectival phrases. Great care is taken with pronoun reference.

Vocabulary Control
At **Intermediate Level** there is a basic vocabulary of approximately 1600 words. Help is given to students in the form of illustrations which are closely related to the text.

Glossary
Some difficult words and phrases in this book are important for understanding the story. Some of these words are explained in the story, some are shown in the pictures, and others are marked with a number like this: ...[1]. Words with a number are explained in the Glossary.

Contents

Life in America 1913–25

At the time of this story, New York was the most modern and fashionable city in America. Writers, actors, businessmen and millionaires lived in New York.

Rich people went to the theatres and cinemas. They ate in expensive restaurants and they wore expensive clothes. They drank champagne in bars. They went dancing and listened to jazz music. The most expensive and fashionable places in New York were 42nd Street, 5th Avenue and Broadway. 57th Street was in a poorer part of the city.

The cinema was very popular. Movies were made in California, on the west coast of America. Film stars were very rich and many people wanted to act in the movies.

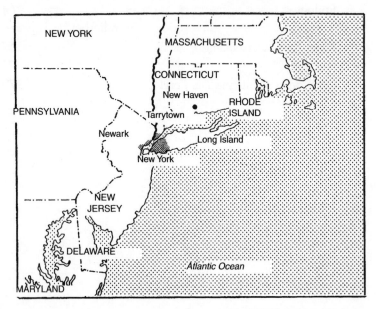

1

Anthony Patch in New York

It was a sunny October day in 1913. Anthony Patch was happy to be in New York again. Anthony smiled as he walked along 52nd Street. His blue eyes looked at everyone and everything. He was very pleased to be in New York.

Anthony smiled again. Anthony was thinking of money– his grandfather's money. Old Adam Patch was going to die soon. Then Anthony would be rich. He would have millions of dollars.

Adam Patch was ill, but he was not dead yet! Anthony was on his way to visit him now. As usual, Anthony arrived late. His grandfather was waiting impatiently[1].

'I'm pleased to hear you're better, Grandfather,' Anthony said. Adam Patch looked at his watch.

'Train late?' the bad-tempered[2] old man asked. Then, 'Sit down, sit down,' he said.

The two men, one old and ill, the other young and handsome, looked at each other.

'Now you're back in America, you must do something,' the old man said. 'I've worked hard all my life. It's time you started to work.'

'I'm thinking of becoming a writer,' Anthony said.

'A writer? Write? Write what?'

'Well, sir, a history. A history of the Middle Ages[3].'

'The Middle Ages?' the old man repeated. 'Why write about the past? Why write about Europe? You're an American. Why don't you write about your own country?'

'It's time you started to work.'

'Well, sir, I've lived in Europe so much . . .'

The old man laughed. 'And I don't call *writing* work,' he said. 'Do you really think you can write?'

'Well, yes, I do,' Anthony replied. 'But, of course, there will be a lot of reading to do first.'

'Didn't you do enough reading at Harvard[4]?' Adam Patch said. He looked at his watch again.

'Well, young man,' he said, 'why don't you go home and start writing?'

Anthony stood up. 'You're right, Grandfather. I have got a lot of things to do. I'll come back again in a few days' time.'

When he was outside on the street again Anthony Patch relaxed[5]. Perhaps he would write – one day! But old Adam Patch was looking ill. He might die soon. And then, Anthony would be a rich man.

That evening, Anthony walked out of his apartment[6]. He looked handsome in evening-dress. He walked slowly down Fifth Avenue to the Ritz-Carlton Hotel.

A short man with fair hair was waiting for him.

'Hello, Anthony Patch!' he called. 'How is old Adam's grandson? Are all the girls still chasing you? It's only the money they want, you know!'

Anthony sat down.

'Hello, Dick. Where are we going tonight?'

'What about dancing? Or going to the theatre?'

'The theatre!' Anthony repeated. 'Perhaps I'll write a play. After I've written my book, of course. And then . . .'

At that moment, a waiter brought them the menu. The two young men began to discuss what they would eat and drink.

Hours later, back in his apartment, Anthony was smoking a cigarette. He sat in the dark by the window. A clock struck one o'clock. In the distance, there was the noise of the traffic on Fifth Avenue. But in this apartment in 52nd Street it was quiet. Anthony liked New York. But, without friends, it could be a lonely place.

Anthony turned away from the window and walked slowly into his bedroom. He smiled as he looked at the soft, red carpet and the large, comfortable bed.

It was a fine apartment. It cost a lot of money. The money came from what his mother had left him when she died. He had an income[7] of seven thousand dollars a year. Not very much, perhaps. But, when his grandfather died . . .

Anthony was still smiling, when he fell asleep.

2

Gloria

A month later it was winter in New York. It was the first cold day. Anthony met Dick Caramel again, walking along 42nd Street.

'I've been writing all day,' said Dick. 'My room's so cold. I am trying to write a novel that's going to be a best-seller. How can I write when I'm cold? Come on, we can't stand here.'

'Where are we going?' Anthony asked his friend. 'Shall we walk up to the Plaza and have a drink?'

'The Plaza? That's a great idea,' Dick answered. 'We'll visit my cousin. She always stays there in the winter. Her name's Gloria.'

'Gloria? Gloria what?'

'Gloria Gilbert. Haven't you met her? She's always going to dances. She's a pretty girl, really pretty. And there's not a brain in her head[8].'

But when they got to the Plaza, Gloria was out.

'She's dancing somewhere,' her mother told them. 'She's always dancing. She dances all the afternoon and all night too.'

At that moment, the door opened.

'Here's Gloria!' her mother cried. 'Look, Gloria, we've got visitors, Dick, and this is . . .'

Anthony smiled at the girl and she looked into his clear, blue eyes.

'Anthony, Anthony Patch,' he said.

'Well, hello, Anthony Patch!' Gloria cried. She held out a little hand. Under her fur coat, Gloria was wearing a blue dress, with a white lace collar[9].

Gloria was beautiful. She was shining with beauty. Her golden hair shone like sunshine. Her eyes were grey and very cool.

'Anthony Patch,' Gloria repeated. 'I think that's the best name I've ever heard.'

'And you're the most beautiful girl I've ever seen,' Anthony said. 'Why haven't I met you before?'

On the following afternoon, Gloria and Anthony had tea together at the Plaza Hotel.

Gloria wore a grey coat with fur round the collar. She was slim, like a child, with the small hands and feet of a child.

'Do you want to dance, Gloria?' Anthony asked her.

'Later, perhaps. I'd like to sit and talk now.'

'To talk about yourself?' Anthony asked. 'You love talking about yourself, don't you?'

'Yes, I do,' Gloria said, with a laugh.

'How old are you?' Anthony asked.

'Twenty-two,' Gloria replied. 'How old did you think?'

'About eighteen.'

'Let's both be eighteen,' Gloria said quickly. 'I don't want to grow old. I don't want to get married. I don't want to have responsibilities. But that's enough about me. Tell me about yourself. What do you do?'

'Me? Nothing,' Anthony replied, with a laugh. 'I haven't found anything that interests me. Perhaps I'm lazy.'

'I like lazy men,' Gloria said. 'I like men who are lazy and handsome. I want nice people around me. I want people I can talk to. People who want to talk to me.'

Anthony laughed. 'You like your life, don't you?' he said.

'Sure[10], as long as I'm young and beautiful.'

They looked into each other's eyes.

'Let's dance,' Gloria whispered[11].

In the weeks before Christmas, Gloria and Anthony were always meeting at parties and dances. But when Anthony wanted to see Gloria alone, she was often busy. Sometimes, when they met, she was sleepy and bored[12].

One evening, Anthony and Gloria were sitting together in a crowded café. The music was loud and the lights were bright. People were drinking and smoking. Gloria was happy. She looked around her and said, 'I'm happy here. I'm like these people. They are the same as me.'

'You're a young idiot!' Anthony cried.

'No, I'm not,' Gloria replied. 'You don't know me. I like bright colours and noise. I don't like clever people. I want people near me who are happy. I want people near me who tell me I'm beautiful. I want to enjoy life, that's all.'

'Well, hello, Anthony Patch!' Gloria cried.

Gloria looked at the dancers.

'I know!' she cried. 'I'm going to have a dinner-party. Yes, a dinner at the Biltmore Hotel. You will be there and Dick . . . some girls I know, and Joseph Bloeckman . . .'

'Who's he?' Anthony asked.

'Joseph Bloeckman? He's the moving-picture man[13],' said Gloria. 'He and my father do a lot of business together. Perhaps I will go into films one day. But not yet. I want to enjoy myself first. I want lots and lots of men to fall in love with me.

'Come on, I'm tired of this place. Let's go somewhere else!'

3

At the Biltmore

It was the night of Gloria's party. Anthony, Dick and Joseph Bloeckman were at the Biltmore at eight o'clock.

Joseph Bloeckman was a heavy man of about thirty-five. He had smooth, pale hair and a confident manner[14]. He introduced himself to Dick and Anthony. Then, turning to Anthony he said, 'You're Adam Patch's grandson, aren't you?'

Anthony smiled and nodded.

'He's a fine man,' Bloeckman went on, 'a fine American citizen.'

'Oh, yes,' said Anthony, smiling again. 'A fine man. Doesn't smoke, doesn't drink. Makes money though, plenty of money.'

Anthony decided he didn't like Bloeckman. Why did Gloria like him?

At that moment, Gloria and the two other girls arrived.
The six of them went in to dinner.

Joseph Bloeckman did not dance. He watched the others.
Anthony danced only with Gloria.

'You look very sweet tonight, Gloria,' he said. 'No, not

sweet. You're beautiful.'

'And I think you're charming[15],' Gloria answered.

'We really like each other, don't we!' Anthony laughed.

The music stopped and they went back to their table. Gloria laughed at Bloeckman who was sitting at the table alone.

'Bloeckman never dances,' she said. 'I think he has a wooden leg!' Gloria often made fun of Bloeckman's name. He did not like it, but he smiled and said nothing.

Then the waiter brought champagne. Soon they were all laughing and joking. Gloria sat with a smile on her face as she listened to Bloeckman talk about the movies.

At ten o'clock, Gloria and Anthony were dancing again. After a few minutes, Gloria whispered, 'Dance over to the door. I want to go to the drugstore[16]. I must have some sweets to chew. If I don't, I'll start biting my fingernails. I'm a bit nervous, you see.'

In the drugstore, Gloria spent a long time looking at perfumes. Then, at last, she bought some sweets. Without saying anything, she and Anthony walked slowly along 43rd Street – away from the Biltmore Hotel.

Spring was coming and the night was warm.

'Let's get into a taxi and ride around a little,' Anthony said, without looking at Gloria.

Oh, Gloria! Oh, Gloria!

A taxi stopped and they got in. Now they were together, away from the crowded city. Anthony put his arm around the girl and kissed her sweet, childish mouth. Her face was turned up towards his. It was pale and beautiful in the dark night. There was beauty in Gloria's face. Beauty, but not love. Gloria rested in Anthony's arms. She was light, bright and beautiful.

Now they were together, away from the crowded city.

They passed the dark buildings of New York. They drove past Central Park and then, on, past the Metropolitan Museum. They were moving like a ship through the ocean of the city.

Oh, Gloria! Oh, Gloria!

Gloria said nothing, but her beauty spoke to Anthony. She said nothing, but her silence spoke of love.

'We must go back,' Gloria whispered at last. 'Tell the driver to go back, Anthony.'

In the hotel the air was hot and filled with cigarette smoke.

'Where have you two been?' one of the girls asked.

'To phone my mother,' Gloria said. 'I promised her I'd call.'

Then something happened that Anthony remembered years afterwards. Joseph Bloeckman leant back in his chair. He looked at Anthony in a strange way. Bloeckman looked at Anthony for a long time. But he said nothing. He did not look at Gloria at all.

4

Goodbye, Anthony . . .

It was ten o'clock on Sunday morning. Anthony was sitting in his apartment, thinking about Gloria.

Gloria! He had never met a woman like Gloria. Gloria! He remembered the ride in the taxi – the kiss.

In a dream, Anthony phoned Gloria's hotel. He waited to hear her voice. He held his breath. But Gloria was out. Her mother did not know when she would be back.

Anthony leant back in his chair. He stared at the wall in front of him and thought of Gloria. Where was she now?

At eleven o'clock, Gloria was in a shop. She was looking at the silks and the furs. The air was full of the scent of flowers.

At midday, she was walking along Fifth Avenue. As she went through the doors of the Ritz, twenty pairs of eyes watched her. At one o'clock, Gloria was having lunch – with a man – of course. At four o'clock, Gloria was dancing. Then, after that, taxis, kisses . . .

———

Anthony jumped up from his chair. Why was Gloria out now? He wanted to kiss her again – he wanted to find peace.

Anthony called Gloria again and again. But she did not get back to the Plaza until eight o'clock. And then – she was too busy to see Anthony until Tuesday afternoon.

———

Tuesday was very cold. Anthony called at the Plaza at two o'clock. Gloria and Anthony shook hands. Had Anthony ever kissed her? Did she remember?

'I called you four times on Sunday,' Anthony said.

'Did you?' Gloria sounded surprised.

'I wanted to see you,' Anthony said. 'I wanted to talk to you. I have something important to say.'

'What do you mean? Don't be serious today, please,' said Gloria. 'I don't want to talk. I want to go walking. Come on.'

17

It was very, very cold. It was impossible to talk. Anthony walked faster and faster.

Gloria called out to him, 'Wait for me!'

Anthony looked back. 'I'm sorry. Did I go too fast?'

They started to walk back to the Plaza. Anthony tried to see Gloria's face, but it was covered by her hat.

They went into the hotel. In the elevator[17], Gloria said nothing. She looked in the mirror and pushed a lock of hair under her hat. Gloria's cheeks were glowing from the cold. Her eyes shone. How beautiful she looked!

Gloria! Oh, Gloria!

Anthony followed Gloria down the hotel corridor. He wanted to go home, but he couldn't.

Then Anthony was in the sitting-room, waiting for Gloria to take off her fur coat.

When Gloria came back into the room, Anthony said, 'Bloeckman's a strange man, Gloria. I don't like him.'

Gloria smiled. 'He doesn't like you either,' she said.

'Is he in love with you?' Anthony asked.

'I don't know,' said Gloria. 'Perhaps.'

'Of course he's in love with you,' Anthony said. 'He looked so angry when we came back from the taxi ride.'

'He wasn't angry. I told him what happened.'

'You told him? Why?' said Anthony.

'Why not? I'm not ashamed[18] of anything I do. Anyway, why must we talk about Bloeckman?'

'I suppose you want to talk about yourself, as usual. Aren't you interested in anything else?'

'Not really.'

Anthony stared at the fire. He hated Gloria when she was hard and selfish.

18

Then a strange thing happened. Gloria turned her head and smiled at him. At once, Anthony forgot everything except the beauty of her face.

Anthony moved closer. Gloria lay against his shoulder. She smiled at him as he kissed her.

'Gloria,' he whispered softly.

Was she in love with him? Did she love him as he loved her? Afterwards, he never knew. But for him, it was an afternoon of sweetness, of romance.

An hour passed and the clock struck five. Anthony stood up and pulled Gloria to her feet. He held her tightly. He kissed her again. Her arms dropped down to her sides.

'Don't,' she said quietly.

'I'm very sorry. Won't you kiss me again, Gloria?'

'I don't want to.'

'Perhaps I'd better go.'

Gloria said nothing.

'Then I'll go,' Anthony said. 'If you're tired of me, I'd better go.'

'You've said that before.'

Anthony picked up his hat and coat. With one last goodbye, he walked quickly from the room.

For over a minute, Gloria made no sound. Then she whispered to the fire. 'Goodbye, Anthony – you idiot.'

5

Anthony in Love

Anthony was in love. He knew what he wanted. He wanted Gloria. But she had sent him away. He had lost her.

So what would happen now? Anthony remembered Bloeckman. He was middle-aged and rich. He could give Gloria anything she wanted.

Anthony was madly jealous[19] of Bloeckman. He wanted to kill him. But Anthony was still in love with Gloria. He wanted to marry her. Without Gloria, Anthony knew that his life was worth nothing. How could he get her back?

At last, Anthony decided to leave Gloria alone for a month. He would not phone her. He would not go anywhere where he would see Gloria. But not a month – two months. No, that was too long. Perhaps two weeks?

Anthony finally decided not to see or call Gloria for six weeks. He marked off the days on his calendar. On the ninth of April, he would phone her.

One day, Anthony saw Gloria on Sixth Avenue. She looked happy, beautiful and young. And she was with a man Anthony had never seen before.

The following day, Anthony saw Bloeckman in a bar. He was wearing evening-dress.

'Hello, Mr Patch. Do you come here much?'

'No, not much.'

'Nice bar. One of the best in town,' Bloeckman said. He looked at his watch. 'Well, I must go. I'm going to dinner with Miss Gilbert.'

Gloria and Bloeckman! That night, Anthony could not sleep. He lay awake for hours, mad with jealousy.

———

But Gloria and Anthony met again and the sun was shining. The first thing Anthony said was, 'Oh, you've cut your hair!'

And Gloria answered, 'Yes, isn't it wonderful?'

Short hair became fashionable five years later. But on that day, Gloria looked different from all the other girls – and more beautiful.

Anthony and Gloria walked along Fifth Avenue in the sunshine. They went to the zoo and watched the animals. And Central Park was beautiful. The air was soft and warm.

Anthony asked when he could see Gloria again.

'It would be nice to be together for a whole day,' he said.

'Yes, it would, wouldn't it?'

They had a wonderful Sunday. They sat in Anthony's apartment. The soft, warm air blew gently through the open windows. They kissed and their kisses were sweet.

At six o'clock, they went out to Fifth Avenue. The people were full of happiness and laughter. Anthony told Gloria that he loved her. And she had answered, 'I'm glad . . .'

The following day, Anthony phoned Gloria.

'Gloria, dear, I wish I could see you.'

'You will. Tomorrow night.'

'That's a long time. Couldn't I see you tonight?'

'I have a date[20], but I could break it.'

'Oh, Gloria, I love you!'

Anthony looked very handsome that night. He walked along the corridor to the apartment and knocked. His blue eyes shone. He went into the apartment. Gloria was standing on the other side of the room. As Anthony closed the door,

Gloria gave a little cry and ran towards him. He took her in his arms and they kissed. Her beautiful dress was crushed between them. They held each other in a long, loving embrace.

They held each other in a long, loving embrace.

6

The Wedding

Anthony and Gloria decided to marry in June. Gloria's mother was surprised, but pleased. During the following days, Anthony and Gloria kissed, quarrelled[21], made up, quarrelled and kissed again.

'Oh, Gloria, I love you,' Anthony whispered. But they quarrelled all the time. Then Anthony would say, 'Now Gloria – please let me explain . . .'

'Don't explain. Kiss me.'

'I don't think that's right, Gloria,' Anthony said. 'If we quarrel, we ought to talk about it. I don't like this "kiss and forget".'

'But I don't want to quarrel,' Gloria replied. 'And I think it's wonderful that we can "kiss and forget". Oh, Anthony, when I'm mean[22] to you, I'm sorry afterwards. I don't want to hurt you.'

Then Gloria was in Anthony's arms, crying like a little girl.

Before the engagement was announced[23], Anthony went to see his grandfather.

'Oh, you're going to get married, are you?' old Adam Patch said. 'Are you working?'

'Oh, yes,' Anthony began. 'My book is . . .'

'I mean real work,' Adam Patch said impatiently. 'How much do you save in a year?'

'Nothing, so far . . .'

'So you spend every penny on yourself. And now you've decided that you've enough money for two!'

Anthony became angry.

'Gloria has some money of her own,' he said. 'She has enough to buy her clothes. We'll have enough money. We're getting married in June.'

'Like to have the wedding here?'

Anthony was surprised. He did not want to agree, but he wanted to please his grandfather. He was going to get the old man's money in the end, but it was better to keep the old man happy.

'I'll speak to Gloria about it,' Anthony said. 'I'll see what her family wants. But it's very kind of you, sir.'

'I'm an old man,' Adam Patch went on. 'I think a lot about the past. And the future. You should think about the future, too. You ought to get a job – work harder.' The old man's eyes went hard.

'When I was your age, I'd already ruined[24] three men. Off you go, young man, or you'll miss your train.'

Dick Caramel's book was published just before the wedding. It was badly written, but very successful. Everyone in New York was talking about it.

Gloria told Dick that she had no time to read the book. This made Dick very angry. But Gloria was very busy. Wedding presents arrived every day. Gloria was pleased with each one. Every time a present arrived, she tore off the paper quickly. Then she held up the present, and said, 'Look, Anthony!'

And Anthony answered, 'Yes, pretty, isn't it?'

There were five days to the wedding. Four days. A special train was going to take the guests from New York to Adam Patch's house. Three days. Two days . . .

Wedding presents arrived every day.

It was the night before the wedding. Gloria was ready to go to bed. She opened a drawer by the bed and took out a little black book. It was a diary. She had been writing a diary for seven years. It began with the words: *I'm going to keep a diary for my children . . .* Many of the entries were written in pencil and were difficult to read . . . dances, kisses, the boys and men who had taken her out . . . Micnaei, Marty, Larry – all forgotten names now. What a list! But all that was finished. She was in love now.

Anthony's name first appeared in April. Then, on 24th April, Gloria had written: *I want to marry Anthony. What a wonderful marriage it will be!* And then, on 7th June, she had written: *Was I wrong to make Bloeckman love me? It's true I made him love me. He was very sad tonight. But he doesn't matter now. It's only Anthony and me. Me and Anthony!*

The diary ended here. After a moment, Gloria took a pencil and drew three lines under the last words. Then she wrote THE END in large capital letters. She put the book back in the drawer and went to bed.

Anthony woke up very early in the morning. It was five o'clock. He looked at himself in the bathroom mirror. His face was white.

He looked at the things on the table – important things. There were the railway tickets for the honeymoon in California, the travellers cheques[25], his watch and, most important of all, the wedding-ring. It was made of platinum[26], set around with small emeralds.

The platinum ring was Anthony's third present to Gloria. The first present had been the engagement ring. Then there had been a gold cigarette case. Anthony would be giving Gloria many things now – clothes, jewels, friends and excitement.

And now the wedding-day had arrived. Sunlight began to shine through the window. Suddenly, Anthony laughed.

'My God!' he said to himself. 'I'm nearly married!' And a sudden happiness filled his heart.

7

The Little Grey House

The first six months of their marriage was the happiest time they would ever know. Then, hour by hour, the dream began to fade[27]. Gloria found out that Anthony hated to drive too fast. He was afraid of unusual noises in the night.

Anthony found out that Gloria was very nervous and selfish. And she had a temper. What a temper! She was beautiful and she was spoilt[28]. She had always got what she wanted. For example, food. Gloria was very particular about the food she ate. Some things she liked a lot, and other things she would not eat at all. Once, in a restaurant in Los Angeles, Gloria was given something she did not like. She banged her hands on the table.

'I can't eat this!' she cried. 'I just can't eat it!'

'Then we'll go somewhere else,' said Anthony.

'I'm tired of going to so many places. Why can't I get what I want in this town?'

But after a time, Gloria picked up her fork and began to eat. Anthony relaxed.

Things like this happened all the time. Anthony was often restless[29] and unhappy.

Then, one day, they quarrelled about a laundry-bag[30]. They were staying in a hotel. Gloria was getting dressed to go down to the restaurant. Anthony opened a drawer and said, 'Have you got any clean handkerchiefs, Gloria?'

Gloria shook her head.

'Sorry, I haven't. I'm using one of yours.'

'That's the last clean handkerchief,' said Anthony. 'Isn't the laundry back?'

'I don't know,' Gloria answered carelessly.

Anthony opened the closet[31] door. The laundry-bag was hanging there, full of dirty clothes. He had put them there himself. Beneath the bag, on the floor, were stockings, dresses, night-gowns – all Gloria's laundry.

'Why, Gloria! You haven't sent out the laundry!'   .

'Oh, is it still there?'

'Gloria,' Anthony said quietly. 'I've sent out the laundry in every hotel we've been in since we left New York. But last week, you promised you would do it.'

'Oh, don't be unkind. And don't be cross with your sweetheart.'

So they went down to the restaurant. They bought some new handkerchiefs and all was forgotten.

But two days later, Anthony looked in the closet again. The pile of Gloria's laundry had grown higher.

'You need a servant, Gloria,' Anthony said angrily. Gloria ran to the closet and began to push her clothes into the laundry-bag.

'You need a servant, Gloria,' Anthony said angrily.

'There,' she said. 'Now it's done!'

But the same thing happened again and again. To stop any more quarrels, Anthony sent out the laundry himself.

———

When they got back to New York, they went to Anthony's apartment. They discussed with Dick where they should live.

'I'd like to take Gloria abroad, but there's this damned war[32],' Anthony said. 'So we want a place in the country, near New York. A place where I can write – or do anything I want.'

'But who's going to take me out if you work all day?' Gloria said. 'And how do we find a place?'

'You go out and look for one,' Dick said. 'There are lots of quiet little towns near New York. You can buy a little grey house somewhere . . .'

Gloria jumped up.

'Oh, yes,' she cried. 'A little grey house with trees around it. How can we find one?'

'Well,' Dick said, 'write down the names of seven towns. Then every day this week, take the train to one of them.'

'Trains! I hate trains!' Gloria said.

'I know,' Anthony said. 'If we are going to live in the country, we'll need a car. We'll buy a car. Then we'll drive around until we find a place where we can live.'

———

They left New York the next morning in a cheap, new car After an hour, Gloria was bored.

'Let me drive,' she said.

'Are you a good driver?' Anthony said nervously.

31

'I've been driving since I was fourteen!'

Gloria started the car. As they drove away, Gloria shouted, 'Here we go! Look out everyone!'

'Don't go so fast, the car's new,' Anthony told her.

Gloria smiled and drove a little faster. Later, she turned off the road and went down a side road. Soon, they were lost. They stopped by a signpost.

'Marietta, five miles,' Anthony read.

'Where's that?' Gloria asked.

'I don't know,' Anthony said. 'But let's go on. It's getting late.'

When they reached Marietta, it was almost dark. Then the car broke down. Luckily, they stopped outside a real-estate agent's office[33].

It was dark when the agent showed them the old grey house. Anthony and Gloria both loved it and they rented[34] it for a year.

They stayed the night at the Marietta Inn. They lay awake half the night, making plans. Anthony was going to write his book on the history of the Middle Ages. Gloria was going to read and eat tomato sandwiches. And, of course, they would always have guests in the little grey house.

'We'll have a dog,' Anthony said.

'I don't want a dog. I want a little cat,' Gloria said sleepily. Then they fell asleep.

It was dark when the agent showed them the old grey house.

8

'I Hate You! I Hate You!'

The car was repaired and Anthony and Gloria drove around everywhere. They went out to dances. Their friends came and stayed in the little grey house.

In November, they went back to Anthony's apartment for the winter. They went to theatres and football games. Anthony wrote the introduction to his book.

In April, they went to California. They were invited to all the fashionable parties.

Time passed. Then Anthony found they had spent too much money. So they sold the car. Then he and Gloria went back to the little grey house in Marietta. But Anthony was restless. He started to drink more and more. And Gloria was getting older. She was twenty-four. In another six years she would be thirty. That was terrible!

———

It was June. Anthony and Gloria were visiting friends. It was a hot afternoon. Anthony had been drinking whisky all day.

Gloria finished her sandwich, stood up and said, 'We've got to go, dear, we really must . . .'

Anthony was angry. He finished his drink and said to his friends, 'If Gloria says we must go, then we must go!'

Anthony followed Gloria through the garden and out onto the road. They found a taxi and drove in silence to the station.

But Anthony had decided that, this time, Gloria was not

going to win.

'I don't want to go home,' he said. 'We were having a good time. Let's go back.'

'We can't do that Anthony. Give me the money and I'll get the train tickets,' Gloria said.

'No!' Anthony shouted. 'I don't want to go in that damned[35], hot train!'

Gloria stamped her foot.

'Anthony, I think you're drunk,' she said.

'Not at all. I'm perfectly sober. But I'm not going on that train. We're going back.'

'Well, I'm not,' Gloria said quietly.

But as Gloria turned away, Anthony took hold of her arm.

'This time you're doing what I say,' he said. 'I'm tired of your selfishness.'

Gloria struggled[36] to get away.

'Oh, I hate you! I hate you!' she cried.

By this time, the train had come into the station. People were staring at them. Gloria stopped struggling. She stood perfectly still, glaring[37] at Anthony.

The train left the station. Anthony and Gloria were alone. Anthony had won.

'We'll hire a car and drive back to Marietta,' Anthony said.

Gloria took hold of Anthony's hand with both of hers. She bit him hard on the thumb.

'I won't go, you can't make me go,' she screamed. 'You've killed the love I had for you!'

Anthony wrapped his handkerchief round his bleeding thumb. 'You're going with me,' he said, 'if I have to carry you.'

They drove home in silence. From time to time, Gloria cried quietly.

'Oh, I hate you! I hate you!' she cried.

Anthony was still drunk when they got home. He went straight to his room and fell asleep. It was one o'clock when Gloria came into the room.

'Oh, Anthony, my darling. You don't know what you did to me,' she said softly.

In the morning, Anthony came early into Gloria's room. He knelt down by the bed and cried like a little boy.

The quarrel was never spoken about again. But their love had changed.

———

Soon after this quarrel, Anthony went to see his grandfather. The old man talked of nothing but the war in Europe.

'Well, what have you been doing?' Adam Patch said to Anthony. 'Still writing, I suppose. Why don't you go over to Europe as a war correspondent[38]? I can get you a job with any newspaper.'

'I don't know . . .' Anthony answered slowly. 'I'd like to think about it. It's certainly very kind of you.'

Anthony liked the idea of going to Europe as a war correspondent. He would be away from the world of dances and parties. He would be back with men again.

The train back to Marietta was crowded. Anthony took the last seat on the train. He found he was sitting next to Joseph Bloeckman.

'How's your wife?' Bloeckman asked.

'Oh, fine, fine. Why don't you come out to see us at Marietta sometime? I'm sure Gloria will be delighted to see an old friend.'

When Anthony got home, Gloria was in the garden eating a sandwich. Anthony told her about his grandfather's plan.

'And I think I'll go,' Anthony said.

But Gloria opened her eyes wide with surprise.

'Anthony! Do you really want to go to Europe without me?'

Gloria put her soft arms round her husband's neck. He knew then that he could never leave her.

'But what am I going to do?' Anthony said. 'We've been married a year and we're not doing anything right.

'Grandfather may live for years or he may die tomorrow,' Anthony went on. 'We're spending too much money. I'm almost twenty-seven and my work . . .'

'Your work! Your work!' Gloria repeated. 'You don't work. All you do is sit at your desk and sharpen pencils. You write a sentence or two and then you start reading. That's not work.'

About a week later, they had a visitor – Joseph Bloeckman. Gloria was light, bright and beautiful. She was wearing a yellow dress. She smiled when she saw Bloeckman.

'I'm glad you came. I've decided I want to be a film star. Maybe I could make a million dollars a year!'

'I think you'd do very well, Gloria,' Bloeckman said. 'Come and see me on Wednesday. I'll show you around the studio. I'll tell them to give you a test[39].'

When Bloeckman had gone, Anthony glared at Gloria.

'You don't mind if I have a film-test, Anthony?' Gloria said. 'Just a test?'

'But it's silly,' Anthony replied. 'You don't want to sit around a studio all day!'

'Oh, you make me tired,' Gloria said. 'Do you think I enjoy sitting around here all day?'

'Well, I'll tell you one thing,' Anthony replied. 'If you go into movies, I'll go to Europe.'

'Go then! I'm not stopping you,' Gloria cried.

And then, as usual, Gloria was in tears and in Anthony's arms. They kissed, talked and kissed again.

Finally they both sat down to write letters. Anthony's letter was to his grandfather. And Gloria's letter was to Bloeckman. They had both decided, as usual, to do nothing.

9

The Party

Gloria woke up. For a time, she did not know where she was. Then she heard Anthony breathing heavily beside her. She could smell whisky and cigarette smoke.

Anthony sat up in bed. He stared at Gloria.

'I feel awful,' he said. 'What time is it? Did you put me to bed last night?'

'I don't know,' Gloria replied. 'I thought you put me to bed.'

They were in Anthony's New York apartment. Gloria was tired of the house in Marietta. And Anthony had to get a job.

They had been in New York for six months. In March, Anthony had taken a job as a salesman. He hated the work and after a month, he left the job.

But they needed money badly. So they sold Anthony's New York apartment and rented the little grey house for a third year. But Gloria and Anthony were not happy when they were alone together. They invited people to stay every weekend and sometimes during the week as well.

The weekend parties were all the same – drinking, dinner at a club, then more drinking. They got up late on Sunday mornings. Then they began drinking again.

So the summer went on. The house always smelt of cigarette smoke and whisky. Anthony and Gloria were always tired. But they needed the excitement of the parties.

———

It was a warm evening in August. Outside, the air smelt of summer flowers. Inside the house, there were glasses and ashtrays everywhere. Everyone was shouting. People were dancing to loud music. The phone rang and someone answered it.

'Hello. What? Who? Sorry, I can't hear you. What did you say? Hello, hello. Oh, they've rung off. I couldn't hear a thing.'

By nine o'clock, the music was louder. People shouted at each other, laughed and drank.

Anthony emptied one bottle and opened another.

Gloria was dancing, round and round. The others shouted and clapped their hands.

Gloria danced faster and faster. She slipped and almost fell through the open door.

And there, standing in the open doorway, was – Adam Patch!

The old man's face was hard and angry. He stood there, leaning on his stick. His secretary was standing beside him.

For about two minutes, the noise went on. Then there was silence. Everyone stared at the angry old man by the door.

The secretary spoke to Anthony, 'Your grandfather

And there, standing in the open doorway, was – Adam Patch!

thought he would drive out and see your home. I phoned earlier this evening . . .'

Anthony's face was white. Gloria was staring at the old man with fear in her eyes.

'We'll go back now,' Adam Patch said quietly. And that was all. The old man turned slowly and left the house without another word. Adam Patch hated drink and drunkenness more than anything else in the world.

———

The guests had gone. Gloria and Anthony looked at each other in misery and fear.

'I've got to apologize[40] to my grandfather,' Anthony said.

'He won't accept your apology. He'll never forgive you as long as he lives.'

'But I must try,' said Anthony. 'I must see him. I'll say I'm going to give up drinking.'

'He looked sick,' Gloria said.

'He is sick,' Anthony answered. 'I told you that three months ago.'

'I wish he'd died last week,' Gloria went on. 'The old fool!'

Anthony waited a week. Then, feeling very afraid, he went to his grandfather's house.

The old man was not well. His secretary would not let Anthony into the house.

So Anthony and Gloria wrote Adam Patch a letter of apology. But the letter was never answered.

About a month later, they left the little grey house for the last time.

'I'm so glad to go,' Gloria cried. 'My God, how I hate this house!'

'Don't be angry,' Anthony said. 'We've got nothing now except our love for each other.'

'We haven't got that, most of the time,' Gloria answered.

And so they left the house where their love had changed. The shining and beautiful Gloria went back with her husband to New York.

Anthony tried to rent his old apartment, but the price was too high.

'We've got to find a place to live,' he said. 'We can sell some more bonds[41]. But . . .'

'How much money have we got every month?' Gloria asked quickly.

'Six hundred dollars.'

'Only that?'

'That's right. And we spend about twelve thousand a year.'

'You've got to get a job,' Gloria said. 'And you've got to go and see your grandfather.'

'I know, I will . . .'

———

They rented a small apartment on 57th Street. Anthony read in a newspaper that his grandfather was dangerously ill. Anthony went to see old Adam Patch at once, but the sick man would not see him.

Adam Patch died in November. Anthony and Gloria went to the funeral[42]. Then they waited to hear how much money Adam Patch had left them in his will[43]. A week passed, and Anthony heard nothing.

On the last day of November, Anthony phoned his grandfather's lawyer. Gloria sat listening, biting her finger nails.

'Yes, of course I'm interested,' Anthony said. 'I've heard nothing about the will. I thought perhaps you didn't have my address . . .

'Oh, that's very strange. Are you sure? Well, thanks . . . Yes, I see.'

Anthony put the phone down. He turned and looked into Gloria's wide staring eyes.

'My dearest,' Anthony whispered. 'He did it. He cut me out of his will. There's nothing, nothing . . .'

'He cut me out of his will. There's nothing, nothing . . .'

10

Oh, My Gloria!

The next day, Anthony went to a lawyer.

'I want you to fight my grandfather's will,' he said. 'It must be possible to change it.'

'Who did he leave the money to?' the lawyer asked.

'He left forty million dollars,' said Anthony. 'His secretary got one million and the rest went to some charities[44].'

'Do you know why he cut you out?'

'Well,' Anthony said, 'perhaps it was because of the party. He hated drinking and people enjoying themselves. He came over to see us last summer. There was a noisy party going on. He took one look and went away.'

'And you think that's why he cut you out?' the lawyer asked.

'Well, I don't know,' said Anthony. 'But you must fight this will. The old man wasn't thinking clearly when he made it.'

———

Two months went by. The parties went on – lots of parties. The little apartment always smelt of smoke and whisky. But Anthony and Gloria looked the same.

Gloria was twenty-six, but she looked twenty. Her skin was clear and smooth. Her hair was bright and golden. Wherever she went, people looked at her. She was still beautiful.

Anthony was always well-dressed. His sad face was more

handsome than ever. He had written a few stories. But they were not successful. He soon stopped writing.

Both Anthony and Gloria tried to spend less money, but it was impossible. They were having parties every day.

'While I'm still young, I want to enjoy myself,' Gloria said.

'And after that?' asked Anthony.

'After that, I won't care.'

So they went on spending more and more money.

One day, Bloeckman visited the apartment. When Anthony came in later, Gloria said, 'Would you mind if I went into the movies?'

'What made you think of that again?'

'Bloeckman was here. He said he could get me a job in films. But I've got to start now. They only want young women. Think of the money, Anthony!'

'I don't like the idea,' said Anthony. 'Why did Bloeckman come here again? What do I do? Live on your money?'

'If you don't like the idea,' said Gloria, 'make some money yourself!'

And so the quarrelling went on.

———

In April 1917, America declared war[45] on Germany. The country was now part of the war in Europe.

Anthony tried to join the army, but he failed the medical examination. Anthony and Gloria had been married for three years. The case[46] of Adam Patch's will came to court in September. Anthony lost, but his lawyer appealed against the decision. Anthony and Gloria talked more and more about the things they would do with the money – when they got it. They talked about the places they would visit after the war.

Then, at the end of the summer, Anthony had to go into the army. This time, he passed the medical examination.

The day came when Anthony had to leave New York. He was leaving by train. Gloria was always late. This time she

was almost too late to say goodbye to him. The station was crowded. There were people everywhere. She waved goodbye to Anthony above the heads of the crowd. They were too far away from each other to see the tears in their eyes.

She waved goodbye to Anthony above the heads of the crowd.

This was in October 1917. Anthony was away for more than a year. But he never left America. The war ended the following year.

———

November 1918. Broadway[47] was full of light. The streets of New York were crowded with people, waving and shouting. When Anthony got back to New York, he tried to phone Gloria. But there was no answer.

Anthony hurried to the apartment. He ran from room to room, calling Gloria's name. But she wasn't there.

Then the phone rang.

'Hello, is Mrs Patch there?' a man's voice said.

'No, but I'm looking for her myself,' Anthony said. 'This is Mr Patch speaking. I've just got back.'

'Oh,' the voice said. 'I suppose Gloria's at the Astor, then. At the Armistice Ball[48].'

Anthony put down the phone. Still wearing his uniform, he hurried to the Astor Hotel.

The dance floor was full of people, singing and shouting as they danced. People shouted, laughed and kissed. The war was over!

As the music played, Anthony pushed his way through the crowd. Then he saw Gloria. Her dress was black and her bright, beautiful face was shining. Anthony called her name. Gloria looked up and saw him.

'Oh, my Gloria!' Anthony cried, as he held her in his arms. She kissed him and he felt at peace.

Ten days later, Anthony left the army and came back to live in New York.

11

Oh, My Pretty Face!

And now it was the end of February. As Anthony came into the little apartment, Gloria turned away from the window.

'What did the lawyer say?' she asked.

'Nothing. We'll hear something next month, perhaps.'

Gloria looked at Anthony more carefully.

'You've been drinking,' she said. 'You haven't seen the lawyer, have you?'

'No,' Anthony replied. 'I'm tired of sitting in his office. I met someone and we had a few drinks. What have you been doing?'

'Thinking about how much I want a fur coat.'

'You can have one if you want,' Anthony said slowly. 'But we've spent a lot of money since I've been back.'

'Oh shut up!' said Gloria. 'I'm tired of hearing you complain[49]. You said you wouldn't touch another drink until you got a job.'

'And I'm tired of hearing you complain.'

'Well, what are you going to do about it? You're weak, just weak and you always have been . . .'

They quarrelled like this every day. The winter passed and they went on spending money.

Late in March, Anthony got another job as a salesman. But he hated it. He had to have a drink or two before he could sell anything.

Every morning, Anthony woke up tired, restless and

51

worried. He was not happy until he had a drink in his hand. The rest of the day passed in a dream.

When Gloria complained, Anthony shouted at her, or walked out of the apartment. And every day they had less and less money.

Summer passed and autumn. Then it was winter again. In February, Gloria would be twenty-nine! That was nearly thirty! And what did she have? Nothing. Nothing was left except her beauty. She was still beautiful. So Gloria decided to use her beauty before it was too late.

Seven days before her twenty-ninth birthday, Gloria phoned Joseph Bloeckman. They had not met for five years.

'Can you see me?' Gloria asked. 'It's business. I'm going into the movies at last – if I can. Could you give me a film-test?'

'Of course. I'm glad you've decided to. I think I've got just the part[50] for you.'

Gloria decided not to tell Anthony until she got the part. On the day of the test, she dressed carefully and put on a little make-up. Gloria looked in the mirror. She was a little thinner. But she still looked beautiful.

At the film studio, she was excited by everything she saw. The director[51] told Gloria what she had to do.

'You come into this room,' he said. 'It's your husband's office. The phone rings and you answer it. Your husband's had an accident – he's dead. At first, you can't believe it. Then you fall down in a faint on the floor. OK?'

Then the director's voice was coming from behind the bright, white lights.

'Walk around the office – your husband isn't here – walk around . . .'

At the film studio, she was excited by everything she saw.

Gloria moved. She felt nervous. The phone rang.

'Hello.' Her voice sounded strange. She held the edge of the table, her eyes wide and staring.

'My God,' she cried. 'Oh, my God!'

'Faint!' shouted the director.

Gloria fell on her knees and lay on the floor without breathing.

'All right. That's enough. Thank you.'

Gloria got up and brushed her clothes.

'Terrible, wasn't it?' she smiled nervously.

Bloeckman promised that he would write to Gloria in a few days.

Gloria waited three days. She was very nervous. She went for a walk in Central Park. She looked at her watch every few minutes. When she was a star, she would have a new watch. She would have a new watch and a grey fur coat.

Going into the apartment, Gloria felt sick. Yes, the letter had arrived.

My dear Gloria,

We looked at the test yesterday. The acting wasn't bad, but they want a younger woman.

There is another, smaller part, for an older woman. Perhaps you . . .

Gloria couldn't read any more. She walked into the bed room. She knelt before the long mirror. As Gloria looked at herself, her eyes filled with tears. It was her twenty-ninth birthday.

Yes, her face was thinner. And there were tiny lines at the corners of her eyes. Her eyes! How tired and sad they looked!

'Oh, my pretty face!' Gloria whispered. 'Oh, my pretty face! How can I live without my pretty face? Oh, what's happened to me? What's happened?'

And Gloria lay on the floor and cried and cried.

12

No Love, No Money

A year later, Gloria and Anthony had moved into a cheaper apartment.

Anthony was now thirty-two. He was heavier and less handsome. His mind was slow. The case of Adam Patch's will was still not settled. Anthony could not get a job now. He did not try. His eyes, that had been a deep, clear blue, were now red and weak.

Anthony was drunk most of the time. Anthony and Gloria's friends were tired of paying for meals. They were tired of listening to Gloria and Anthony's endless quarrels. Anthony was drunk every day–either in the apartment or in a bar. Gloria complained all the time. She felt very sorry for herself.

Every night, Gloria put on a lot of face-cream. She was trying to bring back her beauty. And when Anthony was drunk, he laughed at her.

One afternoon, Anthony met Dick Caramel on 42nd Street. Anthony had been drinking whisky all day. Dick looked at Anthony's face and then at his shirt, which was dirty and torn.

'My God, look at yourself,' Dick said. 'You look terrible!'

'. . . Old man's will . . .' Anthony said. 'Lost a lot of money .

'. . people talking about us . . . when we change the will . . . everything all right then.'

'What are you talking about? I can't understand you,' Dick said.

'Well, I'm not saying it all again,' Anthony shouted, turning away.

Dick ran after him.

'Anthony, don't talk like that! Gloria's my cousin and you're one of my best friends. Are you going to get your grandfather's money?'

'Well, maybe. We're still waiting for a decision. The waiting's terrible. It's best if you leave us alone.'

Anthony was tired of talking. Without another word, he turned and walked away.

As time went by, Anthony became worse and worse. If he had no money for a drink, he lay in bed until midday. In the afternoon, he sat in the little apartment for hours, doing nothing. As soon as he had some money, he went out to a bar and got drunk.

Gloria made coffee and prepared meals. In the afternoons, she walked and in the evenings, she read.

One afternoon, when she came home, Anthony was walking up and down nervously.

His eyes, that used to be clear and blue, stared as he said, 'Have you any money?'

'What do you mean?' Gloria asked.

'What I said. Money! Money!' he shouted.

Gloria shouted back – 'Why, Anthony, you must be crazy. I've only got a dollar.

'Anthony,' Gloria said suddenly. 'We can't live like this. Let's sell our bonds[52] and go to Italy for three years. When the money is all gone, we'll just die.'

'You're crazy. Three years? We haven't got enough money to live in Italy for one year. We have to pay the lawyer. Do you think he's working for nothing?'

'I forgot him.'

'I've only got a dollar,' Anthony went on. 'And it's Saturday. I can't sell another bond until Monday. What about Bloeckman? He's always wanted to help you.'

'Oh, he doesn't like me any more. I went to him a year ago.'

'Why didn't you tell me?' asked Anthony.

'You were probably out drinking somewhere,' Gloria answered. 'Anyway, I had a film-test and I wasn't young enough. But that doesn't matter now. We need something to eat. We've got about two dollars between us. That should be enough, shouldn't it?'

Anthony grabbed the money from Gloria's hand.

'No,' Anthony said. 'I've got to have a drink. I'll go and pawn[53] my watch.'

Anthony got up.

'Leave the money with me!' Gloria cried.

Anthony banged the door behind him. On the street, he counted the money. He had enough for a drink. He would pawn his watch afterwards.

–––––

Three hours later, Anthony began walking home. He was so drunk that he could hardly stand. It was dark and all the shops were shut. It was too late now to pawn his watch. Anthony saw that he was outside the Biltmore Hotel. He had an idea. He would have a talk with Bloeckman.

'I want Mr Bloeckman,' Anthony told the doorman. 'Tell him that Mr Patch wants to see him – now!'

A few minutes later, Bloeckman came down the stairs.

'You want to see me?' he asked.

'Yes. How are you, my friend?'

'I'm fine. But I can't stay long. What do you want?'

Anthony glared at Bloeckman. He had forgotten about money now.

'Why didn't you get my wife into the movies?' Anthony asked.

'Look here, Patch,' Bloeckman answered. 'I think you're drunk. Very drunk.'

'Not too drunk to talk to you. I want you to keep away from my wife. Do you understand?'

'You're not drunk, you're crazy,' Bloeckman said. 'I've got to go.'

'Not yet,' said Anthony.

The two men stood looking at each other. Bloeckman was shaking with anger.

'Be careful,' he said quietly.

'Careful? You be careful, you damned . . .'

Bloeckman hit Anthony once on the mouth and twice more on the face.

Anthony fell down, his mouth full of blood.

'Throw him out!' Bloeckman said to the doorman. 'Throw him out onto the street.'

Anthony was pulled to the door. He fell on his hands and knees and rolled over onto his side.

Bloeckman hit Anthony . . .

When Anthony woke up, he was very cold. Every part of his body was painful. And someone had stolen his watch.

He slowly stood up and began walking towards the apartment. Anthony laughed.

'What a night! What a night!' he said.

13

We've Won!

Three weeks later, the case of Adam Patch's will came to an end. It was a cold morning in March. A decision was going to be given that afternoon.

Anthony got out of bed. He began to dress himself slowly. He poured out a glass of whisky and went into Gloria's room. Gloria had been ill in bed for a week.

'How do you feel? Better?' Anthony asked her. 'Are you well enough to go to court this afternoon?'

'Yes, I want to,' Gloria said. 'I'm having lunch with Dick. So we'll go to the court together and meet you there.'

Anthony sat down on the bed.

'God, I'm nervous,' he said.

Dick came for Gloria at twelve o'clock. When they had gone, Anthony stood by the window. The fine weather made him think of Italy. That's where they would go – Italy! A land of sunshine and happy people.

Anthony poured himself a whisky. He drank it quickly and took another. Hardly able to stand, he suddenly saw his face in the mirror.

His face was white. He looked ill. His eyes were red and he looked like an old man. Anthony was thirty-three, but he looked fifty.

With a sudden cry of anger, Anthony threw his glass at the mirror. But the heavy white face and stupid smile were still there.

'I'll kill you, I'll kill you!' Anthony shouted. He picked up a chair and smashed the mirror.

Then he swung the chair round and round, breaking and smashing . . .

Anthony shouted and smashed and shouted again. Then a darkness filled his mind. Something broke inside his head. With one last cry, he fell heavily to the floor.

———

Gloria and Dick came back to the apartment at five o'clock. They called Anthony's name, but there was no answer. They went into the sitting-room and saw the smashed mirror and furniture.

They saw Anthony in his bedroom. He was sitting on the floor. He was looking at hundreds of stamps. They were the stamps he had collected when he was a child. The stamps were lying all round him on the carpet.

Anthony looked up and stared at Gloria and Dick.

'Anthony!' Gloria cried. 'We've won!'

'Don't come in here,' Anthony said angrily. 'I'm busy. I've got to count these stamps.'

'Don't you understand?' Dick shouted. 'You're rich. You've got thirty million dollars!'

Anthony stared at them.

'Shut the door when you go out,' he said.

'Anthony, what's the matter?' Gloria cried. 'What's happened to you? What is it?'

'Go away,' Anthony said quietly. 'Get out now. If you don't, I'll tell my grandfather.'

Anthony held up some stamps. Then he let them fall. They were bright in the sunlight. He laughed softly as the stamps fell silently to the floor.

He laughed softly as the stamps fell silently to the floor.

Epilogue

The big liner[54] was slowly crossing the Atlantic Ocean. The weather was warm and many passengers were walking on the deck.

'That's him,' said a young man to the girl beside him. 'That's Anthony Patch.'

The young man pointed to a man who was sitting in a wheelchair.

'People say Patch went a little crazy when he got his money,' the young man went on. 'That was about five months ago. The other man in the case, the secretary, shot himself. But Anthony Patch doesn't care. He's got the money.'

'She was here a moment ago,' the girl said. 'His wife. She had a fur coat that must have cost thousands of dollars. She dyes[55] her hair and she looks – unclean . . .'

'But she's not bad-looking,' said the young man. 'I wonder what *he's* thinking about. His money, I suppose.'

But Anthony Patch was not thinking about his money. He was thinking about all the bad times he had had. His friends had all left him. Gloria had turned against him. He had had to fight on his own.

Only a few months ago, everyone had been telling him to forget the case and to go to work. But he had known he was right. And when he got the money, of course, all his friends came back again.

Tears came into Anthony's eyes.

'I showed them,' he whispered to himself. 'It was a hard fight, but I didn't give up. I won, didn't I? I won, after all.'

The big liner was slowly crossing the Atlantic Ocean.

Points for Understanding

1

1 When would Anthony Patch be rich?
2 Who was Anthony on his way to visit?
3 What did Adam Patch want Anthony to do?
4 What did Anthony say he was going to do?
5 It was a fine apartment. It cost a lot of money.
   (a)   Where did Anthony's money come from?
   (b)   How much was his income each year?

2

1 What was Dick Caramel trying to do? Why was he finding it difficult?
2 How did Dick Caramel describe
   (a)   Gloria Gilbert's looks?
   (b)   Gloria Gilbert's intelligence?
3 When they got to the Plaza, Gloria was out. Where was she?
4 Describe Gloria Gilbert.
5 'I don't want . . .' said Gloria. What was it that Gloria did not want?
6 What kind of man did Gloria say she liked?
7 What kind of people did Gloria want near her?
8 'I'm going to have a dinner-party,' Gloria said.
   (a)   Where was the dinner-party going to be held?
   (b)   Who was Gloria going to invite?
   (c)   Who was Joseph Bloeckman?
9 What did Gloria say she might do one day?

3

1 Describe Joseph Bloeckman.
2 How did Anthony describe Adam Patch?
3 What did Bloeckman do while the others were dancing?
4 Who did Anthony dance with?
5 'I want to go to the drugstore,' said Gloria.
   (a)   What reason did Gloria give for leaving the Biltmore?

    (b)   What did Gloria and Anthony do when they left the drugstore?

6 'Where have you been?' one of the girls asked. What did Gloria reply

7 Then something happened that Anthony remembered years afterwards. What happened?

4

1 Anthony phoned Gloria's hotel. What did her mother say?

2 Anthony thinks of all the things that Gloria would be doing. What did he imagine she would be doing at –
    (a)   eleven o'clock?
    (b)   midday?
    (c)   one o'clock?
    (d)   four o'clock?

3 Why could Gloria not see Anthony until Tuesday afternoon?

4 Anthony had something important to say to Gloria.
    (a)   Did Gloria want to listen?
    (b)   What did she want to do?

5 'Bloeckman's a strange man,' said Anthony. What did Gloria say in reply?

6 What did Anthony think Gloria wanted to talk about?

7 When did Anthony hate Gloria?

8 'Perhaps I'd better go,' said Anthony.
    (a)   What was Gloria's reply?
    (b)   What did Gloria say when Anthony had gone?
    (c)   What do you think she meant?

5

1 Why did Anthony want to kill Bloeckman?

2 Anthony met Bloeckman. Who was Bloeckman going to have dinner with?

3 They had a wonderful Sunday. Why was it wonderful?

6

1 When were Anthony and Gloria going to get married?

2 They loved one another. But what did they do all the time?

3 'How much do you save in a year?' Adam Patch asked Anthony. What was his reply?
4 What did Adam Patch tell Anthony he should do?
5 How did Adam Patch surprise Anthony?
6 What was everyone in New York talking about?
7 How were the guests going to travel to the wedding?
8 On the night before the wedding, Gloria took a little book out of a drawer by the bed.
   (a)   What was the book?
   (b)   What had Gloria written in it about Bloeckman?
   (c)   What words did she write in the book?
9 Anthony looked at the things on the table.
   (a)   Why do you think he had railway tickets and travellers cheques?
   (b)   What were Anthony's three presents to Gloria?
   (c)   What things would Anthony now be giving to Gloria?

7

1 Then, hour by hour, the dream began to fade.
   (a)   What did Gloria find out about Anthony?
   (b)   What did Anthony find out about Gloria?
2 Two examples are given to show how Gloria was bad-tempered, selfish and spoilt.
   (a)   The first example happened in a restaurant. Describe what happened.
   (b)   The second example happened in a hotel bedroom. Describe what happened.
3 Why did they decide to buy a car?
4 Where did they decide to rent a house?
5 What was Anthony going to do in the little grey house? What was Gloria going to do?

8

1 Where did they stay in November and what did they do?
2 Where did they stay in April and what did they do?
3 Why did they go back to the little grey house in Marietta?
4 Were they happy there? What did Anthony start to do, more and more?

5 In June, they went one day to visit some friends. They had their worst quarrel. Describe the quarrel.
6 What happened to their love after the quarrel?
7 What job did Adam Patch offer to get Anthony?
8 Who did Anthony meet on the train going back to Marietta?
9 Why did Gloria not want Anthony to take the job which Adam Patch had offered him?
10 What did Gloria say Anthony did when he was working?
11 What did Bloeckman offer Gloria?
12 Why did Anthony not want Gloria to accept Bloeckman's offer?
13 Finally, they both sat down and wrote letters.
    (a) Who did Anthony write to? What did he say in his letter?
    (b) Who did Gloria write to? What did she say in her letter?

9

1 What job had Anthony taken? How long had it lasted?
2 What happened at the weekend parties?
3 One evening in August, they were having a party. The phone rang and someone answered it. Then something terrible happened. Describe what happened.
4 Gloria said, 'I wish he had died last week.'
    (a) Who was she talking about?
    (b) Why did she wish he had died last week?
5 What happened when Anthony went to visit his grandfather?
6 What happened when Anthony wrote a letter to his grandfather?
7 Was Gloria sad to leave the little grey house?
8 Why was Anthony thinking of selling more bonds?
9 What two things did Gloria tell Anthony he must do?
10 After Adam Patch's death, they waited to hear from Adam Patch's lawyer. Why did they think the lawyer would want to phone them?
11 Anthony phoned Adam Patch's lawyer. What did the lawyer tell him?

10

1 Why did Anthony think Adam Patch had not left him anything in his will?

2 Gloria was twenty-six. How old did she look?
3 Both Anthony and Gloria tried to spend less. Were they successful?
4 What made Gloria think again of going into the movies? Did Anthony agree with her suggestion?
5 What happened when Anthony tried to join the army?
6 The case of Adam Patch's will came to court in September.
   (a)   Did Anthony win the case?
   (b)   What did Anthony's lawyer do?
7 What did Anthony and Gloria talk about, more and more?
8 Anthony was leaving New York by train, to join the army. He and Gloria were too far apart to see the tears in each other's eyes. Why?
9 Anthony met Gloria again at the Armistice Ball. How do we know that they still loved each other?

11

1 Why had Anthony not been to see the lawyer? What had he done instead?
2 Anthony got another job as a salesman. What did he feel about the job?
3 What did Anthony need each day, before he could feel happy?
4 Seven days before her twenty-ninth birthday, Gloria phoned Joseph Bloeckman.
   (a)   Why did she phone him?
   (b)   How long did Gloria have to wait for the letter?
   (c)   What did she read in the letter?

12

1 Anthony was now thirty-two. How much had he changed?
2 What were Gloria and Anthony's friends tired of?
3 Why could Dick Caramel not understand what Anthony was saying?
4 What did Anthony do if he had no money?
5 'Anthony,' said Gloria suddenly. 'We can't go on living like this.'
   (a)   What suggestion did she make?
   (b)   What was Anthony's reply?

6 Anthony decided to go and pawn his watch. What did he do first?
7 Anthony saw that he was outside the Biltmore Hotel. He had an idea.
   (a) What was the idea?
   (b) Describe what happened.
   (c) What happened to Anthony's watch?

13

1 It was a cold morning in March. What was going to happen that day?
2 What did Anthony do as he was dressing himself?
3 Who was Gloria going to go to the court with?
4 Why did Anthony think of Italy?
5 Why was Anthony hardly able to stand?
6 What did Anthony do when he saw himself in the mirror?
7 Gloria and Dick came back to the apartment at five o'clock.
   (a) What news did they have to tell Anthony?
   (b) What was Anthony doing?
   (c) What did Anthony say he would do if they didn't get out?

Epilogue

1 Where was the big liner?
2 Why were many passengers walking on deck?
3 The young man pointed to a man who was sitting in a wheelchair. Who was sitting in the wheelchair?
4 How did the girl describe Gloria?
5 'I wonder what he's thinking about. His money, I suppose,' said the young man. What was Anthony thinking about?

Glossary

1 **impatiently** (page 5)
an impatient person is a person who does not like waiting. Adam Patch is old and ill. He does not like waiting for anybody.

2 **bad-tempered** (page 5)
a person who is easily made angry is bad-tempered.

3 **Ages** – *history of the Middle Ages* (page 5)
Anthony is thinking of writing a book about life in Europe in the 12th and 13th centuries – *the Middle Ages*.

4 **Harvard** (page 7)
a famous university in America.

5 **relaxed** (page 7)
a person who is not worried or nervous is relaxed.

6 **apartment** (page 7)
the American word for a flat. Apartments are usually several rooms together on one floor of a big building.

7 **income** (page 8)
Anthony's income comes from money left to him by his mother, when she died. This money is banked in the form of government bonds. Bonds are loans to the government. The government pays interest on the bonds, every year. Anthony's income is the interest which he receives.

8 **head** – *not a brain in her head* (page 9)
Dick Caramel does not think that Gloria is very intelligent.

9 **collar** – *white lace collar* (page 9)
a collar is a band of cloth, round the neck of a dress. The collar of Gloria's dress is made from *lace* – a material made from fine, white thread.

10 **Sure** (page 11)
an American expression meaning 'of course'.

11 **whisper** (page 11)
to speak very quietly.

12 **bored** (page 11)
unhappy because you have nothing interesting to do.

13 **man** – *moving-picture man* (page 12)
an important person in the film business. At the time of this story, films were also called moving-pictures or movies.

14 **manner** – *confident manner* (page 12)
    to have a confident manner is the opposite of being nervous or
    worried. Joseph Bloeckman is clever and quiet.
15 **charming** (page 14)
    Anthony had a very pleasant way of talking and behaving.
16 **drugstore** (page 14)
    an American word for a chemist's shop or pharmacy. A shop
    where medicines, perfumes, cosmetics and sweets can be bought.
17 **elevator** (page 18)
    an American word for a lift. A machine to take people up and
    down from one floor to another in large buildings.
18 **ashamed of** (page 18)
    Gloria does not think she has done anything wrong. So she is not
    worried or ashamed of what she has done.
19 **jealous** – *madly jealous* (page 20)
    Anthony does not want Gloria to love anyone else. You are
    jealous when you think the person you love loves another person.
    Anthony is madly jealous – so jealous that it is making him mad.
20 **date** – *have a date* (page 21)
    to have a date with someone is when a man and a woman arrange
    to meet each other. They make a promise to meet and go to a
    restaurant, theatre or a cinema.
21 **quarrelled** (page 24)
    when two people *quarrel*, they disagree about something and
    argue about it. Anthony and Gloria have many quarrels. When
    they stop quarrelling and become friends again, the quarrel is
    made up.
22 **mean** (page 24)
    to be mean to someone is to be unkind to them.
23 **announced** – *before the engagement was announced* (page 24)
    an engagement between two people is a promise to marry each
    other. Gloria and Anthony announce their engagement, by
    putting a notice in newspapers. This notice tells all their friends
    that they are going to get married.
24 **ruined** (page 25)
    Adam Patch was a very successful businessman. He once beat
    three men at business so badly that they lost all their money.
    They were ruined.
25 **cheques** – *travellers cheques* (page 27)
    when you go on holiday, you do not want to take lots of money
    with you. Money can be lost or stolen. But travellers cheques

74

cannot be cashed at a bank, unless you have signed them. They
are not so easily lost or stolen.

26 **platinum** (page 27)

a very valuable, white metal. Anthony has bought Gloria a
platinum wedding ring which has valuable, small, green jewels all
round it.

27 **fade** – *the dream began to fade* (page 28)

when Anthony and Gloria got married, they were very much in
love with each other and very happy. They lived in a dream.
When they got to know each other better, their love began to
fade – it became less strong.

28 **spoilt** (page 28)

Gloria is spoilt because she has always been given everything she
wanted.

29 **restless** (page 29)

a restless person is never still and quiet. They always want to do
something, but they do not know what to do.

30 **laundry-bag** (page 29)

Gloria and Anthony are living in a hotel. Every room in a hotel
has a laundry-bag. People put their dirty clothes in the bag.
When the bag is full, it must be put outside the door of the room.
The hotel staff take the dirty clothes away to be washed and
ironed.

31 **closet** (page 29)

an American word for a cupboard where clothes are kept.

32 **war** – *this damned war* (page 31)

the First World War was fought in Europe from 1914 to 1918.
During this time, it was not easy for Americans to visit European
countries.

33 **office** – *real-estate agent's office* (page 32)

real-estate is an American word for houses or land which can be
bought or sold or *rented*. (See Glossary no. 34 below). The agent's
office is where the business of renting a house is arranged.

34 **rent** (page 32)

to rent a house is to pay money to live in the house for a certain
time.

35 **damned** (page 35)

an expression of anger and disgust.

36 **struggle** (page 35)

to struggle is to fight to get away from someone who is holding
you.

37   **glare** (page 35)
     to glare at someone is to look at them with anger or hate in your
     eyes.
38   **war correspondent** (page 37)
     a war correspondent is a person who works for a newspaper. The
     war correspondent goes to places where a war is being fought and
     writes reports about the war for the newspaper.
39   **test** – *give you a test* (page 38)
     a *film-test* is a test to see how good a person is at acting. A short
     scene is filmed and the person who wants to become an actor
     takes part in the scene. This shows if they are good enough to
     become a film actor.
40   **apologize** (page 42)
     to apologise is to say you are sorry for saying or doing something
     which you now know was wrong.
41   **bonds** – *sell some bonds* (page 43)
(See Glossary no. 7)
     Anthony and Gloria have spent more money than they get from
     the income from their *bonds*. They have to sell bonds in order to
     get more money. This means that their income will become
     smaller and smaller.
42   **funeral** (page 43)
     a ceremony when a dead person is buried.
43   **will** (page 43)
     before someone dies, they write a paper saying what they want to
     happen to their money and property, after their death. Adam
     Patch wrote in his will that he did not want Anthony to get any
     of his money. He *cut Anthony out of his will*. Anthony believes
     that this is wrong. He thinks he should get Adam Patch's money,
     because he is Adam Patch's grandson. Anthony pays a lawyer to
     fight the will. Anthony wants the lawyer to persuade the court
     that his grandfather's money should go to him.
44   **charities** (page 46)
     organizations which help poor people who need food and
     clothing and a place to stay.
45   **war** – *declare war* (page 47)
     in 1914 Britain and France *declared war* on Germany. The war
     lasted from 1914 to 1918. America joined in the war against
     Germany in 1917.

46 *case* (page 47)

a case is argued in a law court. The court decides who is in the right and who is in the wrong. The person in the right wins the case. The person in the wrong *loses* the case. The person who loses the case can disagree. He can *appeal against the decision* and take the case to a higher court and ask the higher court to change the decision.

47 **Broadway** (page 50)

a famous street in New York. It is famous because of the great number of theatres on the street.

48 **Ball** – *Armistice Ball* (page 50)

a special party and dance held when the First World War came to an end in 1918.

49 *complain* (page 51)

to complain is to say angrily that you are unhappy about something.

50 *part* (page 52)

to have a part in a film is to act in the film.

51 *director* (page 52)

a director tells actors what to do when a film is being made.

52 **bonds** – *sell our bonds* (page 57)

(see Glossary no. 7 and no. 41).
Gloria says that they should sell all their bonds and go to Italy and live there until their money is finished. When the money is finished, they should die.

53 *pawn* (page 57)

to pawn a watch or something valuable is to get a loan of money for the watch. You can buy the watch back again, at a higher price.

54 *liner* (page 64)

a large ship which goes across the oceans. In the 1920s, many people travelled between Europe and America on liners.

55 *dye* (page 64)

to dye your hair is to put something on it to change its colour.

Shane *by Jack Schaefer*
Old Mali and the Boy *by D. R. Sherman*
Bristol Murder *by Philip Prowse*
Tales of Goha *by Leslie Caplan*
The Smuggler *by Piers Plowright*
The Pearl *by John Steinbeck*
Things Fall Apart *by Chinua Achebe*
The Woman Who Disappeared *by Philip Prowse*
The Moon is Down *by John Steinbeck*
A Town Like Alice *by Nevil Shute*
The Queen of Death *by John Milne*
Walkabout *by James Vance Marshall*
Meet Me in Istanbul *by Richard Chisholm*
The Great Gatsby *by F. Scott Fitzgerald*
The Space Invaders *by Geoffrey Matthews*
My Cousin Rachel *by Daphne du Maurier*
I'm the King of the Castle *by Susan Hill*
Dracula *by Bram Stoker*
The Sign of Four *by Sir Arthur Conan Doyle*
The Speckled Band and Other Stories by *Sir Arthur Conan Doyle*
The Eye of the Tiger *by Wilbur Smith*
The Queen of Spades and Other Stories *by Aleksandr Pushkin*
The Diamond Hunters *by Wilbur Smith*
When Rain Clouds Gather *by Bessie Head*
Banker *by Dick Francis*
No Longer at Ease *by Chinua Achebe*
The Franchise Affair *by Josephine Tey*
The Case of the Lonely Lady *by John Milne*

For further information on the full selection of
Readers at all five levels in the series, please refer
to the Macmillan Readers catalogue.

Published by Macmillan Heinemann ELT
Between Towns Road, Oxford, OX4 3PP
Macmillan Heinemann ELT is an imprint of
Macmillan Publishers Limited
Companies and representatives throughout the world

ISBN 0 435 27229 2

F. Scott Fitzgerald's second and longest novel was
first published by Scribners in 1922

These retold versions by Margaret Tarner for Macmillan Guided Readers
First published 1989, Reissued 1992
Text © Margaret Tarner 1989, 1992, 2001, 2003
Design and illustration © Macmillan Publishers Limited 1998, 2003
Heinemann is a registered trademark of Reed Educational and Professional Publishing Limited
This version first published 2003

Illustrated by Adrian Hodgkins
Cover by Dolores Fairman and Threefold Design

Printed in China

2007 2006 2005 2004 2003
14 13 12 11 10 09 08 07 06